HISTORY
FROM BUILDINGS

Victorian
Britain

Tim Locke

W
FRANKLIN WATTS
LONDON • SYDNEY

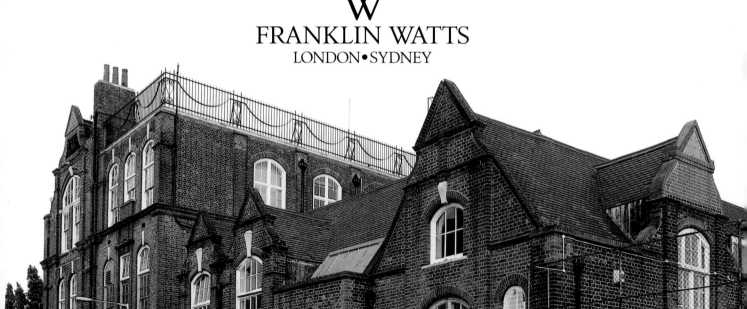

First published in 2006 by
Franklin Watts
338 Euston Road
London NW1 3BH

Franklin Watts Australia
Hachette Children's Books
Level 17/207 Kent Street
Sydney NSW 2000

Copyright © Franklin Watts 2006

ISBN-10: 0 7496 6471 1
ISBN-13: 978 0 7496 6471 8

Dewey Classification: 720.9

Planning and production by
Discovery Books Limited
Editor: Helen Dwyer
Design: Simon Borrough
Picture Research: Rachel Tisdale

A CIP catalogue record for this book is available
from the British Library.

Printed in China

Photo credits:

Front cover top left Discovery Picture Library/Alex Ramsay, top right Highstone Group Ltd, bottom left © 2004 MCC, bottom right Discovery Picture Library/Paul Humphrey, titlepage Discovery Picture Library/Alex Ramsay, 4 Tim Locke, 5 top Glasgow City Chambers/DRS Graphics, 5 bottom Discovery Picture Library/Alex Ramsay, 6 Discovery Picture Library/Alex Ramsay, 7 left Gladstone Working Pottery Museum, 7 right Tim Locke, 8 Alex Ramsay, 9 top Tim Locke, 9 bottom Discovery Picture Library/Alex Ramsay, 10 Discovery Picture Library/Alex Ramsay, 11 top Discovery Picture Library/Alex Ramsay, 11 bottom Tim Locke, 12 top Tim Locke, 12 bottom Discovery Picture Library/Alex Ramsay, 12 top Tim Locke, 12 bottom Discovery Picture Library/Alex Ramsay, 13 National Trust Picture Library/Andreas von Einsiedel, 14 top The Judge's Lodging, Presteigne, 14 bottom National Trust Picture Library/Rupert Truman, 15 left The Judge's Lodging, Presteigne, 15 right Ryedale Folk Museum, 16 top & bottom Discovery Picture Library/Paul Humphrey, 17 top Mike Newman/www.trurocathedral.org.uk, 17 bottom Discovery Picture Library/Alex Ramsay, 18 Discovery Picture Library/Alex Ramsay, 19 top Glasgow School of Art/Eric Thorburn © 2003, 19 bottom Tim Locke, 20 top & bottom © 2004 MCC, 21 Tim Locke, 22 top & bottom Discovery Picture Library/Alex Ramsay, 23 top George Nicol Graphics, 23 bottom Tim Locke, 24 Courtesy of the Crossness Engines Trust, 25 top Elan Valley Visitor Centre, 25 bottom Julian Beeton/Lewisham Hospital, 26 top & bottom Discovery Picture Library/Robert Humphrey, 27 top Highstone Group Ltd, 27 bottom Tim Locke, 28 left Chuck LaChiusa/www.ah.bfn.org, 28 right Fuller Smith and Turner p.l.c., 29 left British Waterways, 29 right Tim Locke.

CONTENTS

The Victorian period lasted 64 years, from 1837, when Victoria became queen, until her death in 1901. During that time Britain changed hugely. The population more than doubled, from 16 to 37 million. Towns and cities spread out across the countryside and were linked by railways. Gas, electricity, water and sewer networks also appeared for the first time.

Even small buildings like this one had elaborate decoration around the windows, doors and drainpipes. This kind of craftsmanship was not so expensive as it is now, because building workers were not very well paid.

Many Victorian buildings are still in use today. Some of the most spectacular buildings in Britain are Victorian, such as large factories, textile mills, hospitals, churches, schools and libraries. Many were designed to impress people. Factories, bridges, waterworks and railway stations as well as grand town halls and theatres were richly decorated.

Coloured bricks

Brickwork was often constructed using colour bricks. What were known as London 'stock' bricks were yellowish grey. In the Midlands and the north bricks were dark red, and in parts of eastern England they were pale yellow. Sometimes more than one colour of brick was used to make a building look attractive.

Building styles

Most Victorian architecture was inspired by older styles. The main ones were Classical and Gothic. Classical buildings like Glasgow City Chambers (right) imitated buildings from the ancient Greek and Roman Empires. Some Victorian buildings copied Italian buildings from the Renaissance period (14th to 17th centuries), when the Italians were themselves copying the buildings of the Roman Empire.

Gothic buildings, such as Manchester Town Hall (below), were built to look like churches and cathedrals from the medieval period (1066–1485). The tops of the arches and windows are pointed and the columns are very narrow. The architecture makes you look up towards the pointed spires.

You can tell that Glasgow City Chambers is in the Classical style because it has thick columns similar to a Greek temple.

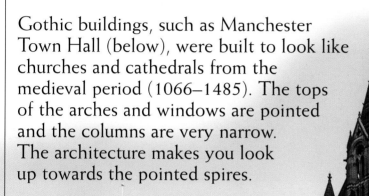

Manchester Town Hall is in the Gothic style and is still one of the first buildings many people notice in the city. There are pointed turrets at the corners but the focus of the building is the huge central clock tower.

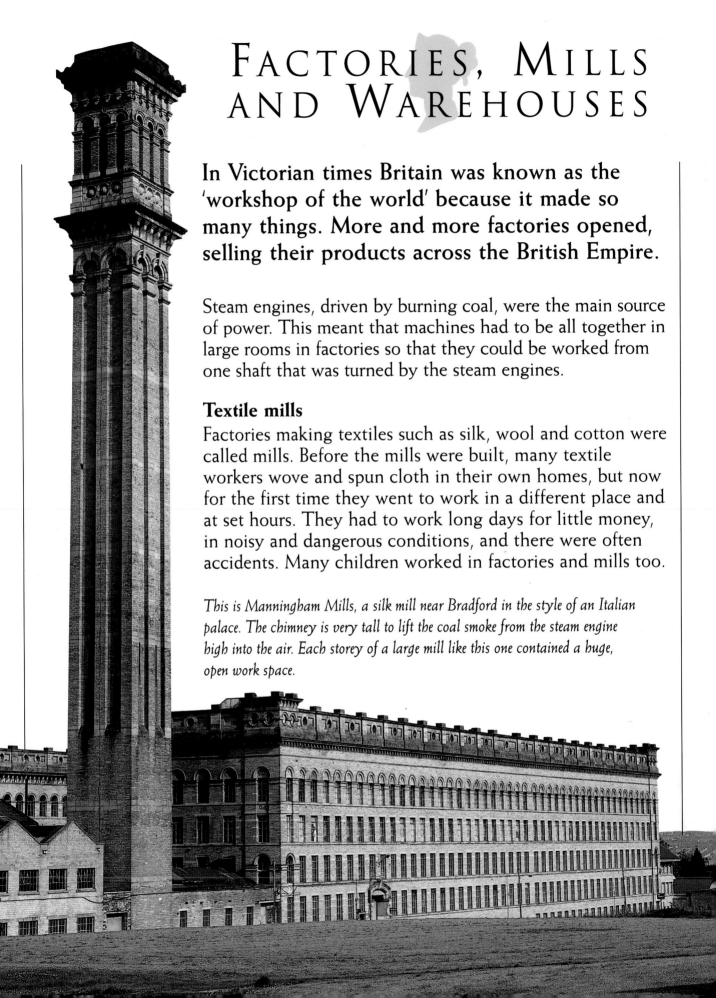

FACTORIES, MILLS AND WAREHOUSES

In Victorian times Britain was known as the 'workshop of the world' because it made so many things. More and more factories opened, selling their products across the British Empire.

Steam engines, driven by burning coal, were the main source of power. This meant that machines had to be all together in large rooms in factories so that they could be worked from one shaft that was turned by the steam engines.

Textile mills

Factories making textiles such as silk, wool and cotton were called mills. Before the mills were built, many textile workers wove and spun cloth in their own homes, but now for the first time they went to work in a different place and at set hours. They had to work long days for little money, in noisy and dangerous conditions, and there were often accidents. Many children worked in factories and mills too.

This is Manningham Mills, a silk mill near Bradford in the style of an Italian palace. The chimney is very tall to lift the coal smoke from the steam engine high into the air. Each storey of a large mill like this one contained a huge, open work space.

In the 'potteries' towns of Stoke-on-Trent in Staffordshire, clay pottery was fired in thousands of brick kilns like these (left). Called 'bottle kilns', because of their shape, they made the air very smoky, and most of them have been demolished.

PAST TO PRESENT

Some Victorian factories, mills and warehouses have been elegantly adapted into shops, museums, offices or flats. Templeton's Carpet Factory in Glasgow (pictured) was built in multi-coloured brick to look like a palace in Venice, Italy. It has been converted into offices.

Warehouses

Beside rivers, canals, docks and railways large buildings called warehouses stored all kinds of goods. Cranes or hoists by the upstairs windows lifted heavy loads up from the ground.

RAILWAYS

In the 1840s railways were constructed all over Britain. It became much easier to transport building materials such as bricks, timber, stone and roof slates than it had been when there were only horses and carts.

Large numbers of men called navvies built the bridges and viaducts, dug the tunnels and created cuttings and raised embankments so that the railway track would be as level as possible, as trains are unable to climb steep hills.

Bridges

The Forth Bridge near Edinburgh in Scotland (below) was made of a new material called mild steel and built in a design based on triangle shapes. This made it strong enough for heavy, fast-moving trains to cross it. Some bridges, such as the Tamar Bridge at Saltash on the border of Devon and Cornwall, were built high up to allow ships' masts to pass beneath.

When the Forth Bridge opened in 1890 it was the largest bridge in the world, and made it much easier for people to travel across Scotland.

Smaller stations, like this one on the Lavender Line in East Sussex, can still be seen all over the railway network. They had a wooden canopy, held up by iron pillars, to give shelter for passengers on the platform. There were comfortable waiting rooms with fireplaces for different classes of traveller, like first-class (the most expensive way of travelling) or women-only. Some Victorian stations today still have more than one waiting room, but everyone can use them and most of the fireplaces have been removed.

St Pancras Station was built in red brick that came by train from Nottinghamshire. The building is decorated with spires and a clock tower.

Stations

St Pancras Station in London (below) was the main station for the Midland Railway and housed the railway company's own hotel. It was built in a Gothic style similar to many medieval cathedrals. Different railway companies owned different parts of the railway network. Impressive buildings like St Pancras Station gave the companies the chance to advertise themselves.

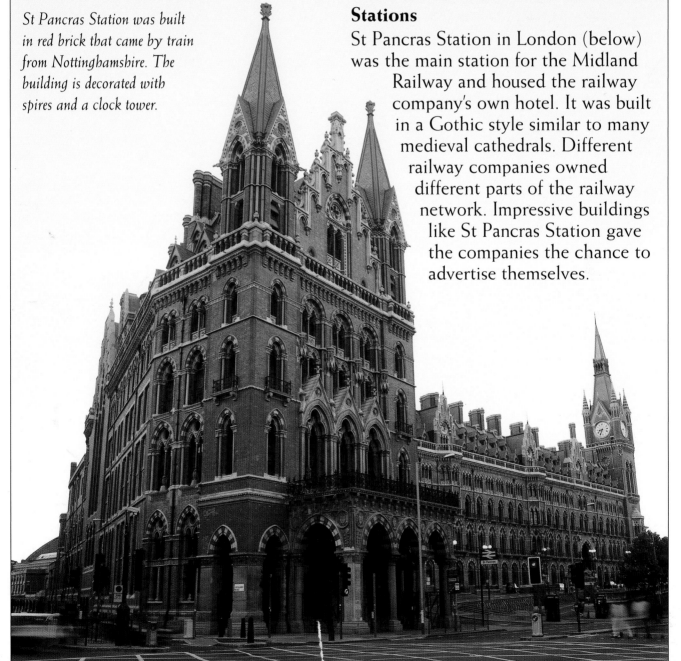

WORKING-CLASS LIFE IN TOWNS AND CITIES

At the beginning of the Victorian age most people lived in the countryside and had jobs to do with farming. But during this period more and more poor people moved into towns and cities looking for work in the new mills and factories.

Many of these people ended up living in slums. These were overcrowded, dirty and badly-built houses with leaky roofs and damp walls. They had no bathrooms. Different families might share one outside toilet and had to go into the street to get water from a pump.

Back-to-back houses

Many new houses were built quickly, in rows or terraces, which were cheap to construct. Some, like these (below) were 'back-to-backs' with a shared inside back wall and no garden in between. Sunlight and air could only come in through the front door and windows.

SEE FOR YOURSELF
Burnley (1), Hebden Bridge (2), Bradford (3) and Huddersfield (4) in Yorkshire are typical mill towns. There are still some factory chimneys and terraces of houses built for factory workers near the mills.

There are factory villages at **Port Sunlight (5)** near Birkenhead in Cheshire and at **Bourneville (6)** next to Cadbury World in Birmingham.

These back-to-back houses in Leeds are still lived in but now they all have inside toilets. Some houses have been extended by building extra rooms in the roof.

By-law houses

In 1875 a law was passed setting special rules for house building, such as having enough windows to light and air the house. Many slums were pulled down, and the new terraced houses that replaced them often had a smaller part that stuck out at the back to allow light into the middle of the house.

Saltaire

These houses at Saltaire, near Bradford in West Yorkshire (right), were built between 1851 and 1871 by Titus Salt, the mill owner. This 'factory village', which had its own hospital and library, is still a very popular place to live.

Titus Salt was not the only rich businessman who was concerned about the living conditions of the poor. The flats pictured below were built by a charity called the Peabody Trust. The trust was founded in 1862 by George Peabody, a rich American banker who wanted to help poor people by giving them good homes.

The houses in Saltaire are much better than most workers' houses of that time. Salt wanted his workers to have well-built homes with gas, running water, a toilet, a coal store and airy rooms.

George Peabody provided 17,000 homes like these in London, all in brick blocks built around courtyards.

HOMES FOR THE MIDDLE CLASS

The middle class included the families of bankers, doctors, shopkeepers, lawyers, clerks and businessmen. Railways made it possible to travel to work, and towns and cities grew outwards along the railway lines. This meant that those who had enough money could live in a pleasant, quiet suburb with trees, parks and clean air.

Suburban living

Middle-class houses in the suburbs were large, with sometimes five or six bedrooms. Families of more than five children were common and there was often a servant or nanny living with them, too.

Cheaper houses were terraced, but richer people had houses that were by themselves (detached), or joined to a neighbour's on one side (semi-detached). A larger suburban house would also have an indoor toilet and bathroom with running water, a kitchen and a separate scullery for washing clothes and dishes.

Semi-detached houses

These two semi-detached houses are in the suburbs of London. On the ground and first floor they have bay windows which stick outwards to bring extra light into the rooms. These houses also have decorations in plaster around the doors and windows.

THE ENTRANCE

Often a house had a path of decorative tiles leading to a front door that had stained glass and a brass letter box, as in this picture. In the front garden, there would be an iron cover over a hole leading to the coal cellar, so when coal was delivered it could be dropped straight down into the cellar.

The windows of these houses open by sliding the panes of glass up or down. They are called sash windows. The house on the right has a smooth grey slate roof like it would have done in Victorian times but the roof on the left has been replaced with modern tiles.

Middle-class interiors

Most Victorian rooms would look very cluttered to us with furniture, mirrors, potted ferns, ornaments and pictures. In the late 19th century a very different kind of interior became popular. William Morris developed a style called Arts and Crafts. This had lighter colours and simpler hand-made furniture and ornaments. William Morris designs are still popular today.

In this room at Wightwick Manor, West Midlands, the curtains and the tiles on the fireplace are patterned with designs based on natural shapes like leaves and flowers.

LIFE IN THE COUNTRY

In the country a lot of the land belonged to wealthy people living in large houses on country estates. In the Victorian age there was a new class of very rich people who had made their money from factories and businesses. They built their own new country houses in many styles.

Grand interiors

Houses like Cragside (below) had grand rooms that were meant to impress guests. They had high decorated ceilings and oil paintings on the walls. Dining rooms had long polished tables, and there might be a ballroom for dancing and a billiard room for the men to play a game after dinner.

This dining room, in the Judge's Lodging in Presteigne, Wales, is heated by a large open fire. Heavy velvet curtains keep out the draughts from the windows.

Like the dining room on the opposite page, this servant's kitchen and dining area is in the Judge's Lodging in Presteigne, Wales. There was no rich decoration in this room, unlike in the main dining room, as only the servants used it.

This restored farm worker's cottage in North Yorkshire has thick walls and small windows. The copper warming pan on the wall to the left was filled with hot coals and used for heating the beds.

Down in the kitchen

Kitchens in these houses were large rooms with stone floors, copper pans that needed polishing, large scrubbed wooden tables for preparing food, and coal-fired ranges for cooking food. Kitchens could be a long way from the dining room, so the servants carried hot food with special silver covers over it. Sometimes a lift called a 'dumb waiter' carried food and dishes up or down, between the kitchen and dining room. Country houses needed many servants as there was so much work to do.

Country cottages

Poor people working on farms and country estates usually lived in simple cottages (like the one above right) made of local building materials. There would be an open fire or cooking range and a few ornaments or pictures downstairs and perhaps one or two bedrooms upstairs.

SEE FOR YOURSELF
Here are some country houses that give an excellent idea of how the rich lived in Victorian times.
1 Cragside House, Northumberland
2 Brodsworth Hall, North Yorkshire
3 Wightwick Manor, West Midlands
4 Castell Coch, South Glamorgan
5 Tyntesfield, Somerset
6 Standen, East Sussex

CHAPELS, CHURCHES AND MEMORIALS

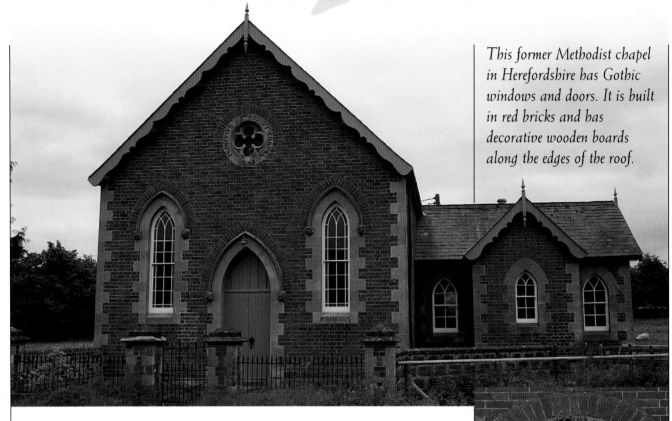

This former Methodist chapel in Herefordshire has Gothic windows and doors. It is built in red bricks and has decorative wooden boards along the edges of the roof.

The Christian religion was very important to the Victorians. Many towns and villages across the country have churches that were built in Victorian times. Some are grand buildings where hundreds could worship, but many are small chapels where a handful of the faithful could gather. The pictures on these pages show two very different types of Victorian Christian places of worship.

This tiny window on the chapel is dated 1866. You can often see a date on Victorian buildings.

Chapels

Chapels, like the one pictured here, were plain, simple places of worship built by Christian groups like the Methodists and the Baptists, who opposed gambling and the drinking of alcohol. Many chapels were built in industrial cities, and in Wales and Cornwall.

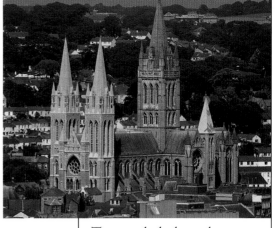

Churches

Most Victorian churches are in Gothic style, with pointed arches. Inside they often have richly coloured stained-glass windows, decorative floor tiles and long wooden pews for people to sit in. The Bible is often kept on a brass stand called a lectern. In Victorian times, many medieval churches were repaired or rebuilt, and it can be difficult to tell today if some churches are medieval or Victorian.

Burial grounds

There was little space left in churchyards to bury the dead because of the expansion of towns and cities. New burial grounds called cemeteries were set up on the edge of towns and laid out like public parks. The most expensive burial plots might have the best view, such as the splendid tombs (below) built for wealthy people in Glasgow. At first bodies were buried, but later on it became fashionable to cremate (burn) the dead.

Tombstones can tell us a lot about how people lived and died in Victorian times. Families were often quite large but many children died young from diseases. Mothers often died young, too, usually from giving birth.

Truro cathedral was begun in 1880. It was the first cathedral to be built in Britain since St Paul's in London more than 200 years before. Truro cathedral is in the Gothic style, just like a medieval cathedral.

In this Glasgow cemetery very rich people were buried in a monument with columns, or with a statue of themselves in the style of ancient Greek and Roman monuments.

IMPROVING THE MIND

During the Victorian period people realised more and more how important it was for all children to learn to read and write, and for everybody to know something about science, art, music and literature. Many of the schools, universities, libraries and art galleries we have today were built then.

Educating children

At first, many children from poor families had to work on farms and in factories and could not go to school. But from 1870 many new schools called board schools were built (like the one below), and children aged 5 to 10 had to attend. By 1891 education was free. Although boys and girls had lessons together, they had separate entrances and playgrounds, and had to sit on opposite sides of the classroom.

Bonner Street School was originally a board school in London. It was solidly built in brick, with high ceilings. The large windows gave plenty of light but were too high to look out of during lessons, so pupils would not be distracted by what was outside.

The architect Charles Rennie Mackintosh designed the Glasgow School of Art (left) at the end of the Victorian period. It is built of Scottish sandstone with wrought-iron windows and railings. The large windows let in plenty of light – ideal for the students painting there.

Once they left school, maybe aged 12 or 13, children could go to evening classes at a night school or mechanics' institute. The Glasgow School of Art (above) was one of the specialist colleges open to students after they had left school.

Educating adults

Some wealthy industrialists wanted to help citizens learn about the world, and gave money to build new concert halls, libraries and art galleries. Frederick Horniman, a tea trader, collected objects from around the world and built the Horniman Museum (right) for everyone to see them free of charge.

The curvy architecture of the Horniman Museum in London is in a late Victorian style called Art Nouveau, which copies shapes from nature like trees and plants.

RED BRICK UNIVERSITIES

At the beginning of Victoria's reign, only men who were members of the Church of England could go to university. Most of them studied religion, Latin and Greek at Oxford or Cambridge. The new Victorian universities that opened in industrial cities during the Victorian age taught new subjects like science, and gave women and members of other religions the chance to be students. Even today these universities are still called 'red brick universities', as many of them were built of red brick.

Before the Victorian age, working people did not have much free time or leisure. They worked on Saturdays and mostly spent Sundays in church or resting at home. From the 1850s factory workers had Saturday afternoons off, and Bank Holidays were introduced in 1871. There was also one week in the summer when the factory closed down and many workers went on holiday.

The Lord's grandstand is designed to give everyone a good view. Each row of seats is higher than the one in front.

Sports grounds

People also started to attend organised sports events. Factory workers could watch a football or cricket match after working on Saturday mornings. Lord's cricket ground in London (pictured here) is one of the sports grounds opened in Victorian times.

The players' balcony at Lord's has an elaborate wrought-iron railing and the decorations are in a carved red brick called terracotta.

Theatres

There were no televisions or cinemas in Victorian times, but many people loved going to the theatre. Music halls had comedy acts, with songs and magicians, and were very popular. Victorian theatres were colourful places, decorated in reds and golds, with velvet curtains. The cheapest seats were right at the top. They were said to be 'up in the Gods', and often had a separate entrance.

Seaside holidays

Now that people could get to the seaside easily by train, seaside holiday towns, like Llandudno in north Wales (below), grew. There were cheap boarding houses and grand hotels to stay in, as well as iron piers for people to stroll along and bandstands on the seafront where musicians sat and played.

SEE FOR YOURSELF

Many Victorian theatres remain in use. These are some of the best preserved of them.

1 Royal Lyceum Theatre, Edinburgh
2 Gaiety Theatre, Douglas, Isle of Man
3 Grand Theatre, Blackpool
4 Theatre Royal, Nottingham
5 Grand Theatre, Wolverhampton
6 Richmond Theatre, Richmond-upon-Thames
7 Palace Theatre, London
8 Devonshire Park Theatre, Eastbourne

These hotels on the seafront at Llandudno are covered with a painted cement called stucco. This protects the bricks or stones underneath and can often be seen in seaside resorts.

21

WORKHOUSES, PRISONS AND THE LAW

Many large workhouses and prisons were built in the Victorian age to house people who had no work or who had committed crimes. In both types of institution living conditions were extremely unpleasant.

Workhouses in a similar style to this one in Andover became a common sight all over Britain. Many were turned into hospitals later on.

Workhouses

Workhouses were places where orphan children and poor people who were unemployed or too old or sick to work were sent. People dreaded going to the workhouse as it felt like being in prison. They had to wear a uniform and do hard, boring work.

Prisons

The Victorians designed new prisons to stop criminals mixing with each other. Each prisoner had a separate cell, with wooden planks for a bed. He had to work hard and was not allowed to talk. The idea was to make prison as unpleasant as possible, to put the prisoners off committing more crimes.

Wormwood Scrubs prison gate (left) is built like a castle, to look forbidding and stern. The prison is still in use today, but prisoners are no longer kept apart.

At courtrooms, like this one in Inveraray, the judge sat high up on a big seat like a throne. The accused person was put in a dock, perhaps surrounded by bars. In big courtrooms there was an upstairs gallery for the public to sit in.

Police stations

The national police force was established in 1829, just before Victoria became Queen. Many police stations were built across the country during Victoria's reign. They were in different styles but always in prominent positions so that everyone could see them.

SEE FOR YOURSELF

Yorkshire Law and Order Museums, Ripon (1)
A Victorian prison cell, courtroom and workhouse.

Lincoln Castle (2)
A Victorian prison and prison chapel.

Southwell Workhouse (3)
Now a museum about workhouse life.

Judge's Lodging, Presteigne (4)
A grand house where judges stayed with a courtroom next door.

After 1861 blue lamps like this one (left) in Penge, London, were placed outside all police stations to identify them easily, except for Bow Street in London, which was white. This was because Queen Victoria often visited the opera house nearby, and said the blue reminded her of the blue room where her husband Albert died.

SICKNESS AND THE GREAT CLEAN-UP

Diseases such as diarrhoea, dysentery, cholera and typhoid killed many people in Victorian times. These diseases spread fastest in the crowded conditions of the new cities. At first people did not understand why, but later doctors discovered that dirty drinking water was to blame.

Sewer systems

In Victorian times, London doubled in size but there were no proper drains at first. For many people, the toilet was just a wooden seat built over a hole or cesspit in the ground. In the crowded towns the toilets often overflowed into the street. A lot of toilet waste, or sewage, ended up in the River Thames, yet people were still using the river for their drinking water.

In 1858 an engineer called Joseph Bazalgette was employed to build special tunnels called sewers to carry the sewage to the east of London. This helped to make the river much cleaner and reduce disease. Sewers were also built in other cities.

This is Crossness, one of the three pumping stations that worked the London sewers. The architect used a very grand style, to celebrate one of the biggest engineering projects ever in the city.

Clean water

In the 1890s Birmingham City Council constructed four great dams (above) in mid-Wales to supply clean water to Birmingham, 118 kilometres away. It was high up enough for the water to flow to Birmingham without needing to be pumped. The reservoirs still supply clean water to Birmingham.

Hospitals

If you became ill and had enough money in early Victorian times, you would probably pay a doctor to treat you at home, because hospitals were dirty and crowded. Later a nurse called Florence Nightingale convinced people it was important to have cleanliness and fresh air in hospitals. The new Victorian hospitals like Lewisham (below) had large windows and well-ventilated wards with high ceilings and iron beds that were easy to clean.

Craig Goch dam in the Élan Valley, Powys, was built at the end of the Victorian age. The narrow valleys of mid-Wales were easy to build dams across to create lakes or reservoirs.

This hospital in Lewisham, London, was built using yellow and red brick, with the red bricks making shapes like Classical columns. The little tower on the roof is called a cupola and is just for ornament.

SHOPS AND COMMERCE

Department stores first appeared in Victorian times. They would have been very exciting places to visit, with everything you needed under one roof. Banks and post offices were also built in every town and city.

The owners of these shops look after their Victorian details very well. They are in Llandrindod Wells, a Welsh spa town where people came to drink the spring water.

Small shops

Compared to today's supermarkets, Victorian food shops were smaller and more specialised. Butchers' shops had meat hanging on hooks, and bakeries baked their own bread in large ovens. Many foods, like tea, raisins, sugar and biscuits, were bought loose, by weight, so there was a weighing scale on the counter. Counters were made of marble because it was very easy to clean.

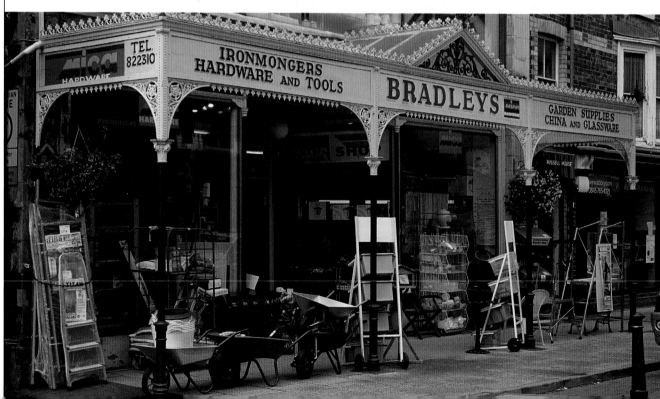

ART NOUVEAU

In the second half of the Victorian period, from about 1890, a totally new style called Art Nouveau ('new art' in French) was invented. This was inspired by shapes from nature, like tree trunks and flowers. There are very few buildings in this style in Britain, but you can see the typical Art Nouveau curvy flower shapes in the tiles and stained glass that decorate this butcher's shop in Shoreham, west Sussex.

Covered markets

Some of Britain's covered markets are spectacular Victorian buildings with decorative ironwork. Special covered shopping streets or arcades like this one in Leeds (above) made shopping more comfortable.

Banks and post offices

Richer people who could afford to save money had bank accounts. Banks were built in a solid, impressive style to give people confidence that their money was safe there. Most town centres today still have a large Victorian post office. As more people learned to read and write, many more people sent letters.

VICTORIAN BUILDINGS
ALL AROUND US

If you go into almost any town or city in Britain you will find Victorian architecture. Town halls, post offices and banks are lined up along straight streets laid out in Victorian times. In the countryside you can see grand houses, hotels and estate cottages.

Restoration

Until the 1970s Victorian houses were rather unfashionable and many were demolished. But now people like them because they are usually well built with large rooms. Some have lost their Victorian details, like tiles and stained glass, but you can buy modern copies.

Many pubs have been restored in a Victorian style with dark wood counters, brass lamps, velvet seats and decorative glass.

PAST TO PRESENT

Some Victorian banks have now been turned into pubs, like this one, the Old Bank of England in the City of London. It was built in an Italian style with Classical columns. Inside it has more columns, three brass chandeliers and a high plaster ceiling.

The decorations in this pub are in Art Nouveau style. The pictures are of monks because the pub was built on the site of an old priory or monastery.

Protecting Victorian buildings

Some of the most interesting Victorian buildings are now protected from demolition by law. They are known as Listed Buildings. The National Trust was set up in 1895 to protect special areas of countryside and historic buildings. Now it looks after some Victorian properties too.

PAST TO PRESENT

These houses are in a similar style to Victorian terraced houses but they were built in the 1990s. They have modern comforts like central heating and double-glazed windows. Notice how the front gardens are now used for parking.

This unusual structure is Anderton Boat Lift in Cheshire. It was built in 1875 to lift canal boats from one level to another. The boats float in a tank that is lifted up with them. After many years of neglect the lift has been restored recently and is working again.

TIMELINE

1837   Victoria becomes queen at the age of 18.

1838   The first photographs are taken.

1840   Postage stamps are introduced for the first time.

1840s   Many railways are built across Britain.

1850   Factory workers are allowed to have Saturday afternoon as a holiday.

1851   The Great Exhibition opens in Hyde Park, London, in a building called the Crystal Palace. In Winchester the first public library in Britain opens.

1856   Henry Bessemer invents a process making it cheaper to mass-produce steel, used for railway lines, steam ships and factory engines.

1858   Joseph Bazalgette begins to build the London sewer system.

1862   The world's first underground railway is opened, from Paddington to Farringdon in London.

1869   Girton College in Cambridge University opens as the first women's college in Britain.

1876   Alexander Graham Bell invents the telephone.

1878   Electric street lighting appears in London.

1880   A law is passed making it compulsory for all children to go to school.

1895   In Birmingham, the first motor car factory in Britain opens.

1901   Queen Victoria dies and the Victorian age comes to an end.

GLOSSARY

architecture the style in which a building is designed.

Art Nouveau a new style of decoration and architecture invented around 1890, based on natural curving shapes inspired by trees and flowers.

billiards a game played with a cue and three balls on a cloth-covered table.

British Empire countries that were ruled by Britain in the Victorian Age, such as India, Canada, Australia and New Zealand.

Classical a style of architecture based on buildings from the Greek and Roman periods, like temples and amphitheatres. Classical buildings have heavy columns.

country estate the farmland, park and buildings owned by a country house.

embankment a long bank of earth on which a railway is built above the normal ground level.

Gothic a style of architecture based on buildings from the medieval period, like churches and cathedrals. Gothic buildings have pointed arches, vaulted ceilings and often pointed spires.

scullery a room next to the kitchen used for washing clothes and dishes.

slate a kind of rock that can be split to make roof tiles. Victorian slates are dark grey and usually came from Wales.

suburb an area of middle-class housing near the edge of a city, from where people could travel to work in the city centre.

viaduct a long bridge with a series of arches that carries a railway over a valley.

Places to Visit

Albert Dock, Liverpool
www.albertdock.com
A Victorian dock with warehouses converted to restaurants and galleries.

Black Country Living Museum, Dudley
www.bclm.co.uk
Victorian and later buildings from the industrial Black Country have been gathered together by a canal to make a village, with craftsmen and costumed demonstrators, shops and factories.

Cardiff Castle, Cardiff, Wales
www.cardiffcastle.com
A castle with amazing Victorian rooms, full of colour and beautiful detail.

Gladstone Working Pottery Museum, Stoke, Staffordshire
www.stoke.gov.uk/ccm/navigation/leisure/museums
A Victorian pottery, with its original kiln and office, housing displays about pottery making.

Glasgow School of Art, Glasgow, Scotland
www.gsa.ac.uk
Begun at the end of the Victorian period, this building by Charles Rennie Mackintosh is in a Scottish version of a style called Art Nouveau that uses ideas from Scotland and Japan. You can visit several other of Mackintosh's buildings in and around Glasgow.

Houses of Parliament, London
www.explore.parliament.uk
An early Victorian building designed in Gothic style by Charles Barry and Augustus Pugin.

Inveraray Jail, Argyll & Bute, Scotland
www.inverarayjail.co.uk
An early 19th-century prison that is home to a museum where you can see the courtroom, cells, 'New Prison' of 1848 and 'airing yard'.

Ironbridge Gorge Museums, Shropshire
www.ironbridge.org.uk
The birthplace of the Industrial Revolution in the 18th century. This exciting, huge museum includes Blist Hill Victorian Town, the Broseley Pipeworks where clay tobacco pipes were made from the 1880s and the Jackfield Tile Museum in a tile factory built 1871–74.

Museum of Welsh Life, St Fagans, near Cardiff
www.museumwales.ac.uk/en/stfagans
Buildings from all over Wales, including some Victorian ones, have been rebuilt here as a big outdoor museum.

Osborne House, Isle of Wight
www.english-heritage.org.uk
Queen Victoria's favourite house, where she spent most of her life. It has hardly changed since she died there in 1901.

Ruddington Framework Knitters' Museum, Nottinghamshire
www.rfkm.org
A restored factory where socks were knitted by machines called 'frames'. It is surrounded by a group of buildings that included preserved and furnished workers' cottages and a chapel.

The Necropolis, Glasgow, Scotland
www.glasgownecropolis.org
A spectacular cemetery with impressive marble monuments commemorating industrialists and other successful people.

Welsh Slate Museum, Llanberis, Gwynedd
www.museumwales.ac.uk/en/slate
Victorian workshops where slate was taken for many of Britain's buildings. You can watch craftsmen working with slate, tour the iron and brass foundry and loco shed, and see the largest working waterwheel in mainland Britain.